TASTY MEALS

BY EDNER PICKETT MITCHELL

AuthorHouse™
1663 Liberty Drive
Bloomington, IN 47403
www.authorhouse.com
Phone: 833-262-8899

This book is printed on acid-free paper.

ISBN: 978-1-4520-7074-2 (sc)

Print information available on the last page.

Published by AuthorHouse 04/27/2021

authorHOUSE®

INTRODUCTION

I am writing this little book, not as a nutritious, dietician, nor doctor, but as a mother and grandmother that have prepared meals for her family throughout the years. Meals that I have tried to balance as healthy and tasty for the family while making sure they ate in moderation to promote good health always. In addition, meals that are light on the wallet.

The meals that I have put together compliments each other while giving the family nutrients, hunger satisfaction and extra money to treat the family to an ice cream cone or movie. What a wonderful feeling to have extra money in the wallet after a visit to the supermarket. Especially with so many people becoming unemployed and our Nation, seem to be slipping into a recession along with some of our children slipping into the obesity mold.

Not to mention meals that are cooked/prepared in the home in which you can control what type of seasoning is used.

How many times have you as the one in charge of preparing meals for the family has boggled your mind for what food would go good with this or that? Meals that the whole family would benefit from as being healthy, soothing to the eyes and tasty to the taste buds. In addition, foods that will make you feel full rather than bloated and hungry again within an hour or less.

Some of you may say that you do not eat some of the foods listed in this book, or say my children want eat it. You may say also that it is fatting. Studies have shown that eating is all about moderation, which is also a way of eating for life.

For those of you that eat such foods as pinto beans, turnip or collard greens; you would boil the beans with oil and vinegar; and the greens with turkey parts not pork. Also, you may use cooking oil along with grounded or crushed red pepper and salt if desired.

If you fry, some of your foods, then use canola or olive oil. Place cooked foods on a paper towel for oil to soak out.

BREAKFAST:

Let us gear up our choices and taste for the first meal of the day.

- Scrambled eggs, grits, bacon slices, sausage patties/links, ham or bologna with a slice of toast topped with butter/margarine and your favorite jelly or jam spread on top.
- Homemade biscuits; bacon/sausage; fried salmon patties and heated corn kernels with a little sugar and butter/margarine.

- Pancakes topped with your favorite syrup; served with sausage patties and scrambled eggs.

- Homemade biscuits; cooked rice and bacon slices.

- Homemade biscuits; fried beefsteak with gravy and steamed white or brown rice.

- Homemade biscuits; bowl of cooked oatmeal and bacon slices.

- Of course there are mornings that you may just want a bowl of your favorite cold cereal and milk; or a bowl of hot cereal; ex(oatmeal, grits, cream of wheat or rice)
  For a more tasty cereal meal, you may add fruits, such as bananas, raisins and strawberries.

LUNCH:

Given the time of the day that you ate such a hardy breakfast, you may only want a peanut butter and jelly sandwich. (better, know as P & J). A hotdog with your favorite chips, tuna fish sandwich, peanut butter on your favorite crackers or slices of bread. Ham, turkey, bologna or spam sandwich topped with your favorite condiments. Cold bologna is good with wheat or white crackers, or a slice of bread with the condiment sandwich spread. Your favorite cheese on crackers, melted or as is. Cheese on a slice of bread is also very tasty.
The children may only want a bowl of their favorite cold cereal, goldfish or cheez-it crackers or just a piece of their favorite fruit. Of course, teenagers and adults may enjoy this light snack as well.

.

DINNER/SUPPER:

Pork and beans can be used with so many dishes (choose your own brand and flavor)

- Pork and beans (heated) served with boiled cut up hot dogs added to beans, boiled cabbage, spinach or broccoli.

- Pork and beans (heated) served with fried salmon patties and your choice of green vegetables.

- Pork and beans (heated) served with turnip greens, macaroni and cheese, along with a cooked pot roast, pork chops and sweet potatoes. (fried or baked)

- Pork and beans (heated) served with collard greens, macaroni and cheese, along with barbecue chicken, sweet potatoes. (fried or baked)

- Pork and beans (heated) served with baked ham and potato salad. (home made or bought)

- Pork and beans (heated) served with fried catfish and coleslaw. (home made or bought)

- Suggested bread: home made cornmeal bread or jiffy mix(with the exception of the catfish meal.) This taste better with slices of white or wheat bread.

- Dessert: (peach, cherry, sweet potato, pumpkin or banana pie)

MORE TASTY MEALS FOR DINNER/SUPPER:

- Pinto beans (cooked) served with boiled hotdogs and coleslaw (topped with a slice of your favorite cheese)

- Pinto beans (cooked) served with a cooked roast and coleslaw. (a slice of your favorite cheese)

- Pinto beans (cooked) served with baked barbecue chicken/pork chops (fried or baked) and yes coleslaw (home made or your favorite bought one) you guessed it your favorite slice of cheese.

- Pinto beans (cooked) served with baked ham and coleslaw. Your favorite brand of cheese.

- Black-eyed peas (cooked) served with baked ham, potato salad (home made or your favorite bought one) coleslaw and again your favorite slice of cheese.

- Bread recommended to go with the beans and black-eyed pea meals is cornmeal.

- Chile made with ground beef or turkey meat. Add pinto beans and serve with crackers.

- Desserts: (baked yellow cake with your favorite frosting or plain), pound cake, chocolate cake or gingerbread and applesauce.

OTHER TASTY MEALS:

- Spaghetti (cooked) served with ground beef or turkey meat added to the sauce or just plain. Hotdogs on the side with a serving of coleslaw and your favorite cheese.

- Spaghetti (cooked) served with fried, baked or grilled catfish and coleslaw. Each serving of spaghetti topped with your favorite brand of cheese.

- Frozen or fresh green beans (cooked) served with a baked or mashed potatoes and fried salmon patties.(pink or jack mackerel)

- Frozen encore steaks (cooked) or steaks freshly prepared. (Broiled/grilled or baked) Served with mashed potatoes and gravy along with a tossed salad topped with your favorite salad dressing or use your favorite brand of mayonnaise. (That's right mayonnaise better know as "mayo")

- Mixed and steamed vegetables served on a bed of cooked white or brown rice, if desired.

- Boiled cabbage, served with frozen or fresh corn, (cooked) canned heated beets and frozen or fresh okra.(boiled)

- Fried beef liver with gravy served with steamed white rice and homemade biscuits or your favorite canned ones. Add a serving of canned peaches or fruit cocktail on the side.

- Fried or baked chicken with gravy served with steamed white or brown rice and homemade biscuits or your favorite canned ones.

- Fried or baked pork chops with gravy, served with steamed white or brown rice and homemade biscuits or your favorite canned ones.

There are times when you or your family may be in the mood for sandwiches and soup, or just a sandwich and chips, use your choice of slices of white or wheat bread, hamburger or hot dog buns. (Meat of your choice)

- Tuna salad sandwich with pork and beans and your favorite chips.

- Fried or cold bologna with sandwich spread on your bread, mayonnaise or mustard; served with a side of pork and beans and your favorite chips.

- Boiled, oven baked or fried wieners (if fried or baked, slice in half vertically). Use your favorite brand served between a slice of bread or bun, spread with mustard or ketchup. (both if desired) I would like for you to try a little coleslaw along with mustard and ketchup on your hot dog. (yummy)

- Ground beef or turkey meat (cooked on your George Foreman grill, baked in oven, fried in electric frying pan or frying pan on top of stove eye,) You can then place your meat between two slices of your favorite bread or bun topped with mayonnaise, mustard, lettuce, tomatoes and onions. (Served with pork and beans and chips of your choice for that satisfying hunger feeling.)

- Two slices of toasted bread filled with a slice of cheese and topped with mayonnaise served with a side of pork and beans or your choice of soup.

- Left over meat from your baked ham, chicken, turkey or roast etc. may be used to create your favorite sandwich. You may choose your own type of condiment and bread.

- Left over chili may be used on your favorite tortilla chips and topped with lettuce, tomatoes, salsa, sour cream, taco sauce. and cheese,

MORE TASTY MEALS:

- Grilled or broiled steaks and a tossed salad

- Grilled or broiled steaks with mashed white potatoes topped with green peas. (your choice of dinner rolls or garlic bread)

- Pot roast and vegetables cooked in your oven, crock-pot or slow cooker. Served with a piece of corn meal bread or muffin. The bread will give you a more filled and satisfying feeling.

- Your favorite broiled or baked fish served with green beans and white mashed potatoes.(your choice of dinner rolls)

- Ground beef or turkey meat loaf served with frozen steamed mixed vegetables or create your own fresh vegetables.(your choice of dinner rolls or a slice of corn meal bread)

TASTY MEALS FOR VEGETARIANS:

- Boiled cabbage and heated canned beets.

- Pinto beans, white beans, black beans or black eyed peas cooked with oil, vinegar, crushed or ground red pepper and salt. If desired. Served with coleslaw and corn meal bread. Beans topped with your favorite slice of cheese. (taste yummy)

- Mixed vegetables such as carrots, zucchini, green bell peppers, green onions, green beans, yellow squash, red bell peppers celery, corn, green peas etc.(quantity of each vegetable is used at your discretion) and may be seasoned to your taste with salt and black pepper, teriyaki, soy, sweet and sour sauce and hot mustard. Steamed white or brown rice may be used as a bed for the vegetables to give a more tastier taste.

- Green bean casserole along with a can of heated corn or boiled corn on the cob.

- Mashed white potatoes topped with green peas. A slice of garlic bread will make this meal more tasty and filling.

- A plate of collard or turnip greens served with a baked sweet potato or yams, a side of macaroni and cheese and a slice of corn meal bread or muffin.

- Spinach (cooked) served with a side of vegetarian beans.

- Tossed salad topped with your favorite salad dressing or mayonnaise and served with your favorite fruit on the side.

- Peanut butter and jelly sandwich (p& j) or just peanut butter on your favorite slice of white or wheat bread.

- Peanut butter on your favorite crackers.(white, wheat, ritz or graham)

- Tomato soup served with a grilled cheese sandwich or just cold cheese on your favorite crackers or a slice of bread.

- Your favorite slices of bread with mayonnaise and banana slices.

- Your favorite slices of bread filled with your favorite ketchup.

- Your favorite slices of bread filled with just your favorite mayonnaise.

- Bowl of vegetable chili with pinto beans added and served with crackers. (Why not add a slice of cheese or shredded?)

MEALS FOR THE LIGHT EATERS:

> ➤ You may want to eat just a small portion of the meals that appeal to your taste buds.

> ➤ Tossed salad.

SPECIAL OCCASION MEALS:

Oven roasted or smoked turkey served with corn meal dressing, green peas, green beans, green bean casserole, hot wings(dipped in ranch dressing), devil eggs, and cranberry sauce (canned or freshly made) Serve with hot home made or bought rolls to compliment this meal.

- You can use chicken or ham in place of turkey for the above meal.

- You might want to throw in a side of turnip or collard greens along with a macaroni and cheese dish.

BEVERAGES RECOMMENDED ARE:

- Tea (hot or cold) a piece of lemon or lemon juice added if desired(sweet or non sweet)
- PUNCH(homemade or bought)
- Favorite soda
- Coffee
- Lemonade
- Juice (your choice)
- Milk
- Water

JUST FOR FUN:

WHY DO I?

As I go through life I find myself doing things that cause me to ask my self "Why Do I" as I am sure many of you have done or do.

- ✓ Why do I hold the toothpaste in one hand while I brush my teeth with the other?
- ✓ Why do I close my eyes while brushing my teeth?

- ✓ Why do I have a wastebasket in my bedroom if I hate to put trash in it? I would rather walk to the bathroom or kitchen and place it in that one?

- ✓ Why do I have a food processor to make kitchen tours easier but rationalize in my mind the cleaning of it?

- ✓ Why do I have a cutting board but hate to get it dirty.

- ✓ Why do I have a stove but hate to use it for cooking, I am afraid I may spill something on it or in the oven?

- ✓ Why do I buy items just because the word SALE is attached to it, knowing good and well I don't need it?

- ✓ Why do I have a car but hate to drive it in the snow and rain hating to get it wet or a spot of dirt on it? Knowing that this is one of the reasons why I have a car and not a bike so that I can stay cool, dry and warm.

- ✓ Why do I find myself driving with my mouth open?

- ✓ Why do I have a house with an attached garage and park my car outside?

- ✓ Why do I have a room that I call the LIVING ROOM but only sat on the nice furniture a few and rare occasions?

- ✓ Why do I have nice silver, crystal and chinaware but never use it?

✓ Why do I say what I am not going to do but find myself doing it any way?

✓ Why do I put off what can be done today for tomorrow?

✓ Why do I worry about what others think of me? (If I keep to myself, I am talked about; and if I associate with others, they still find something to talk about.)

✓ Why do I let someone or others dictate to me my worth?

✓ Why do I tell my child or children this is the last time I am helping you with a problem but end up helping any way.

✓ Why do I yell at the microwave when I have set a cook time of one minute?

✓ Why do I ask the almighty GOD for guidance and end up doing my own thing?

❖ Now that you have an earworm of "Why Do I" ringing in your ears…How will you handle it?

❖ Why not try these tasty foods? You and Your family may not want fast food for at least 2 weeks after recognizing the good and energetic feeling within your body. You will also be surprised of the extra money your wallet or purse has in it.

HELPFUL HINTS:

To preserve a head of cabbage longer, wash well and cover completely with wax paper
And place in a plastic freezer bag before storing in your refrigerator vegetable box.

To keep the refrigerator door handle clean longer, place a kitchen towel on it.

Baking soda may be used as an underarm deodorant. (Dampen under the arm before applying.) It can be used also for whiter and brighter teeth by wetting your toothbrush before placing the baking soda on it to brush.

For a recipe: send an email to tastymealsplus@gmail.com

I was born and raised in Rural Madison Alabama on a farm where there was plenty of land to grow a vegetable and fruit garden. Being the seventh child, I grew up watching my divorced mother try to feed eight children ranging in ages from fifteen years down to three months old. All that I saw and can remember is my older siblings and myself when I became of age to be of help, is planting and harvesting the beautiful big red tomatoes, okra, turnip greens, collard greens, corn , beets, green beans, green peas, cabbages, onions and so many more things that grow in gardens. During the summer months, my mother would can some of the gardens produce along with such fruits as apples, peaches, blackberries and different jellies. My mother had only a small freezer box within the refrigerator, which is why most of the garden produce was preserved in jars.

Meats such as ham and bacon were covered with salt for preserving and kept in a place called a "smoke house". For other meats, my mother and older brothers would go hunting and fishing for food to enhance the vegetables and fruits. The family thought it was a luxury, just to have a little piece of chicken, fish and not to mention a piece of meat that we called "beefsteak" on our plate.

Even though I married and moved to Huntsville, Alabama with my own family and now reside in Illinois, these foods are still a preference in mine and my children's daily meal planning.

Printed in the United States
by Baker & Taylor Publisher Services